Thinking Critically:
Police Powers

Other titles in the *Thinking Critically* series include:

Thinking Critically:
Police Powers

Andrea C. Nakaya

ReferencePoint
Press®

San Diego, CA

For more information, contact:
ReferencePoint Press, Inc.
PO Box 27779
San Diego, CA 92198
www.ReferencePointPress.com

Picture Credits:
All charts and graphs by Maury Aaseng
10: David T. Foster III/TNS/Newscom

LIBRARY OF CONGRESS CATALOGING-IN-PUBLICATION DATA

Name: Nakaya, Andrea C., 1976– author.
Title: Thinking Critically: Police Powers/by Andrea C. Nakaya.
Other titles: Police Powers
Description: San Diego, CA: ReferencePoint Press, Inc., 2018. | Series: Thinking Critically | Includes
    bibliographical references and index.
Identifiers: LCCN 2017021328 (print) | LCCN 2017029967 (ebook) | ISBN 9781682822708 (eBook)
    | ISBN 9781682822692 (hardback)
Subjects: LCSH: Police—United States—Juvenile literature. | Police administration—United
    States—Juvenile literature. | Police misconduct—United States—Juvenile literature.
Classification: LCC HV8139 (ebook) | LCC HV8139 .N35 2018 (print) | DDC 363.2/30973--dc23
LC record available at https://lccn.loc.gov/2017021328

Contents

Foreword

"Literacy is the most basic currency of the knowledge economy we're living in today." Barack Obama (at the time a senator from Illinois) spoke these words during a 2005 speech before the American Library Association. One question raised by this statement is: What does it mean to be a literate person in the twenty-first century?

E.D. Hirsch Jr., author of *Cultural Literacy: What Every American Needs to Know*, answers the question this way: "To be culturally literate is to possess the basic information needed to thrive in the modern world. The breadth of the information is great, extending over the major domains of human activity from sports to science."

But literacy in the twenty-first century goes beyond the accumulation of knowledge gained through study and experience and expanded over time. Now more than ever literacy requires the ability to sift through and evaluate vast amounts of information and, as the authors of the Common Core State Standards state, to "demonstrate the cogent reasoning and use of evidence that is essential to both private deliberation and responsible citizenship in a democratic republic."

The *Thinking Critically* series challenges students to become discerning readers, to think independently, and to engage and develop their skills as critical thinkers. Through a narrative-driven, pro/con format, the series introduces students to the complex issues that dominate public discourse—topics such as gun control and violence, social networking, and medical marijuana. Each chapter revolves around a single, pointed question such as Can Stronger Gun Control Measures Prevent Mass Shootings?, or Does Social Networking Benefit Society?, or Should Medical Marijuana Be Legalized? This inquiry-based approach introduces student researchers to core issues and concerns on a given topic. Each chapter includes one part that argues the affirmative and one part that argues the negative—all written by a single author. With the single-author format the predominant arguments for and against an issue can be synthesized into clear, accessible discussions supported by details and evidence including relevant facts, direct quotes, current examples, and statistical illustrations. All volumes include focus questions to guide students as they read each pro/con discussion, a list of key facts, and an annotated list of related organizations and websites for conducting further research.

The authors of the Common Core State Standards have set out the particular qualities that a literate person in the twenty-first century must have. These include the ability to think independently, establish a base of knowledge across a wide range of subjects, engage in open-minded but discerning reading and listening, know how to use and evaluate evidence, and appreciate and understand diverse perspectives. The new *Thinking Critically* series supports these goals by providing a solid introduction to the study of pro/con issues.

The Power of the Police

In 2014, eighteen-year-old Michael Brown, who was African American, walked out of a convenience store in Ferguson, Missouri, and was stopped a few blocks away by white police officer Darren Wilson. Brown had reportedly stolen cigarillos from the store. Despite the fact that his crime was minor and he was unarmed, Brown was dead just minutes later—Wilson shot Brown multiple times as the young man tried to run away. The citizens of Ferguson were enraged, and they accused Wilson of murdering Brown. They decried Brown's death as yet another example of how US police officers systematically abuse their power.

However, a grand jury decided not to indict Wilson for the shooting, which set off weeks of protests in Ferguson and across the United States. The incident ignited national debate over whether US police officers inappropriately use their power, and whether police departments need massive reforms. While the Ferguson protests were historic, this was not the first time there had been debate and outcry over this issue. Concern over police powers is a long-standing and contentious topic in the United States.

A Position of Great Power

The police are a vital part of every American community. They play a central role in enforcing the law and keeping the peace. Police work includes tasks such as patrolling the streets, making arrests, investigating crimes, and responding to emergencies. In order for police to do their job well, they must have a strong relationship with the community. Community members extend great power to the police—including the power to arrest certain people. This requires a great deal of trust. Community members must trust the officers that serve them and allow them to do their work; they also must trust that police will use their power for the good of the community and not abuse it. In a 2015 report by the President's Task Force on 21st Century Policing, researchers stressed that the institution of policing is founded on trust. "Trust between law enforcement agencies and the people they protect and serve is essential in a democracy," the authors stated. "It is key to the stability of our communities, the integrity of our criminal justice system, and the safe and effective delivery of policing services."[1]

Police officers must also constantly deal with challenging, threatening situations. There is no doubt that policing is a dangerous profession. In a statement made after two police officers in New York City were killed in 2014, then US president Barack Obama stated, "The officers who serve and protect our communities risk their own safety for ours every single day—and they deserve our respect and gratitude every single day."[2]

> "The officers who serve and protect our communities risk their own safety for ours every single day—and they deserve our respect and gratitude every single day."[2]
>
> —US president Barack Obama

Statistics from the National Law Enforcement Officers Memorial Fund show that being killed while on the job is a real threat for police officers. Over the past decade, more than fifteen hundred law enforcement officers have died in the line of duty; this equates to an average of one death every sixty-three hours.

Public Scrutiny of the Police

Not only can police work be dangerous, but police officers are often subject to public scrutiny of their performance as well. Some think this public scrutiny and the public's lack of trust in the police has made this line of work infinitely more difficult. Russ Hicks, an instructor for the Washington State Criminal Justice Training Commission, says that public attitudes toward the police have changed in recent years. Instead of unquestioningly following police orders, citizens are more likely to question what police tell them. "We're having an informed public out there who are asking 'Why? Hold on a second, before you do that, tell me what's going on here,'" he says. "Officers feel very challenged by that."[3] A recent study also shows that it is more common for citizens to scrutinize the police. In 2016 the National Police Research Platform surveyed almost eight thousand law enforcement officers across the United States. It found that members of the community frequently approach police officers to express their opinions on how these officers are doing their jobs. Researchers found that community members expressed both appreciation and criticism. More than three-quarters of respondents said that a community member had thanked them for their service in the past month, but two-thirds said they had been verbally abused.

The fact that so many Americans now carry cell phones that have cameras has increased the scrutiny of police officers. It has become increasingly common for citizens to capture police activity on camera and use that record to critique police behavior or challenge the police's version of events. Philip Matthew Stinson Sr., an associate professor of criminal justice at Bowling Green State University in Ohio, says this has dramatically changed the conversation and perception of police power

Protesters confront police in Charlotte, North Carolina, in 2016. For police to properly do their jobs, there must be trust between police and members of the public. That trust has been sorely tested in recent years.

and abuse. "Before smartphones made it easier for citizens to record possible malfeasance, the police owned the narrative," he says. "There weren't opposing narratives because a dead man can't talk. Videos have opened a window into police behavior rarely viewed by the public."[4]

While most people agree that some scrutiny of the police is a good thing, critics warn that officers cannot do their jobs properly if the public does not respect them. "Freedom comes with a responsibility to be civil towards our fellow citizens. Respect for law enforcement is a vital part of that,"[5] notes commentator Sanjay Sanghoce. He says that without respect for the police, society would fall into anarchy.

Widespread Disagreement over Reforms

Overall, there is intense debate over the institution of policing in the United States. Some insist that police forces are rife with problems such as corruption and excessive use of force. For example, the American Civil Liberties Union argues, "Drastic changes are needed in our approach to public safety."[6] Yet others contend that problems have been greatly exaggerated by critics and the media. They maintain that the majority of America's police officers do an excellent and fair job.

Views about the state of policing in the United States vary significantly by race. Numerous polls show that African Americans and other minorities are much more likely to believe that there are problems in policing and to report that the police have treated them unfairly. For example, in a 2016 survey of more than two thousand adult Americans conducted by the Cato Institute and YouGov, researchers found that 68 percent of white Americans have a favorable view of the police, but only 40 percent of African Americans do.

Differences in opinion also vary by race within the police force itself. A 2016 survey undertaken by the National Police Research Platform asked almost eight thousand police officers about deaths of African Americans during encounters with the police. Interestingly, 70 percent of white officers said these are isolated incidents that did not indicate a broader problem; however, only 43 percent of black officers agreed with that statement.

A Surprising Lack of Data

While there is indeed widespread debate about whether police abuse their power, a major issue driving the controversy is that no one can answer this question for sure. This is because there is a critical deficit of data about the activities of the police, including how often they use force and even how many people are killed by police officers each year. This lack of information is shocking given the plethora of data in other areas. "Today, it seems like there's a stat for everything," notes CNN reporter Eliott C. McLaughlin. "Want to know the most common offense for which people are incarcerated? No problem. Need to know the percentage of fatal plane crashes caused by pilot error? Easy. The score of every Monday Night Football game since 1990? A breeze. But if you want to know how many times a police officer has killed someone in the line of duty, you're out of luck."[7]

> "Today, it seems like there's a stat for everything. . . . But if you want to know how many times a police officer has killed someone in the line of duty, you're out of luck."[7]
>
> —CNN reporter Eliott C. McLaughlin

This lack of information is due to the fact that there is no system for reporting and tracking such data. According to a 2015 report by the US Bureau of Justice Statistics (BJS), there is widespread variation in the way states collect and report data. This means the BJS does not receive complete information on what police around the country are doing. For instance, the BJS is able to collect data on only about 50 percent of arrest-related deaths. Former Federal Bureau of Investigation (FBI) director James B. Comey explains that without such data, it is impossible to settle debates about the way police use their power: "Without complete and accurate data, we are left with ideological thunderbolts."[8]

While it is difficult to make definitive statements about this issue without accurate data, this has not stopped researchers, politicians, police departments, and the general public from trying. One thing is clear: the topic of police power continues to provoke emotional and heated debate throughout the United States.

Chapter One

Do US Police Abuse Their Power?

US Police Abuse Their Power

- Police corruption is widespread, and many officers are also criminals.
- Police frequently use excessive force against those they are sworn to protect.
- As a profession, policing has gotten safer, so claims that officers need to use force to protect themselves are unjustified.
- The widespread use of stop-and-frisk tactics violates the civil rights of citizens.

The Debate at a Glance

US Police Do Not Abuse Their Power

- The majority of police officers act with integrity.
- The use of force is a necessary part of policing.
- Stop-and-frisk tactics are a constitutional and effective way to reduce crime.
- Citizens' lack of respect and compliance is the cause of most violent conflict between the police and civilians.

US Police Abuse Their Power

"Officer misconduct is a very real problem facing Americans."

Sean Everett, "Abuse by the State: Police Brutality Statistics," *Progressive Spring*, July 16, 2014. http://progressivespring.com.

Consider these questions as you read:

1. How persuasive is the argument that police officers are too quick to use force? Which pieces of evidence provide the strongest support for this perspective, and why?
2. Do you think that stopping citizens without proper cause violates their civil rights, or does it help police find evidence of criminal activity? Explain your reasoning.
3. Do you agree that studying crimes committed by police officers is a good way to evaluate police integrity? Why or why not?

Editor's note: The discussion that follows presents common arguments made in support of this perspective, reinforced by facts, quotes, and examples taken from various sources.

In 2015 Michael Slager, a police officer in North Charleston, South Carolina, stopped a fifty-year-old driver named Walter Scott for a taillight violation. While there is disagreement over the exact details of their encounter, the fact that the incident ended in tragedy is undisputed. A bystander with a cell phone captured video of Slager shooting eight times at Scott, who was unarmed. Scott was shot as he was running away from Slager, who struck him multiple times in the back and killed him. The fact that Scott had no weapon, was at least 15 feet (5 m) away from the officer, and was running from him when he was shot indicates that Scott posed no threat to Slager—the shooting was completely unjustified. The Scott murder is another example of the serious problem of police abuse in the United States.

Police Frequently Use Excessive Force

Scott is by no means the only victim of excessive force. According to Campaign Zero, an organization that works to reduce the use of force by America's police, excessive force is common. It estimates that more than one thousand Americans are killed by police officers every year. The organization reports that at the time of death, almost 60 percent of these victims were not carrying a gun, nor were they engaging in behavior that should even require police intervention. According to the organization Mapping Police Violence, one of these victims was Kris Jackson, who was twenty-two and climbing out a window when he was shot by police. His girlfriend says that she did not even hear the officer tell him to stop before he shot Jackson. Another was Terrance Kellom, who was only twenty when he was shot in his own home by officers. Kellom's father insists that he was unarmed. In these and too many other cases, lethal force was completely unnecessary.

When officers are too quick to use force, minor incidents can quickly escalate into unnecessary deaths. One example comes from Oklahoma, where an interaction between state troopers and thirty-five-year-old Nehemiah Fischer ended in death. The original incident was minor: Fischer's pickup truck had been stranded by flooding, and police simply warned Fischer to abandon the truck and get to safety. However, it was dark and the rushing floodwater was noisy, and Fischer and the troopers got into some kind of argument. Fischer became angry and shoved one of the troopers; the trooper's partner responded by shooting Fischer. According to Rosa Brooks, formerly of the US State Department, Fischer's death could have been avoided if the officer had responded in a way that did not involve force. "Technically, the shooting was justifiable," acknowledges Brooks. "But like the deaths of . . . so many others, it could likely have been prevented if police had been less quick to resort to lethal force."[9]

In response to such critiques, many officers say that policing is a dangerous job; some insist they need to use force to protect themselves. However, statistics reveal that policing has actually become less dangerous in recent years. Investigative reporter Radley Balko has researched violence against police officers and has found that as a profession, policing has become increasingly safer since the 1960s. "Assaults on police officers have been dropping . . . which means that not only are fewer cops getting killed on the job, people in general are less inclined to try to hurt them," says Balko. "Yes, working as a police officer is still more dangerous than, say, working as a journalist. (Or at least a journalist here in the U.S.) But a cop today is about as likely to be murdered on the job as someone who merely resides in about half of the country's 75 largest cities."[10] Balko's research suggests that police officers overestimate the danger they face while working and also incorrectly assume that force is needed against the people they encounter.

Police Corruption Is Rampant

Excessive force is not the only way police officers abuse their power. Some officers are corrupt and intentionally break the rules they are supposed to follow; they look out for their own interests rather than protecting the members of their community. The American Civil Liberties Union (ACLU) reports that corruption is a serious problem among US police: "While many police departments and officers make concerted efforts to operate within the rules, police corruption persists."[11] The ACLU is not alone in its assessment; a 2016 Cato Institute/ YouGov survey of more than two thousand Americans ages eighteen and older found that members of the public also worry about police corruption. In fact, nearly half—49 percent—said that they agree with the statement that "most police officers think they are above the law." According to the survey's administrators, "Americans are . . . unconvinced that most police officers have integrity."[12]

> "While many police departments and officers make concerted efforts to operate within the rules, police corruption persists."[11]
>
> —American Civil Liberties Union, an organization that works to defend constitutional rights

Such corruption often goes unrecognized because few records are kept on police misbehavior. In addition, law enforcement officers are also reluctant to speak up when fellow officers break the law. This was one of

Recent Killings of Black Men Are Part of a Broad Pattern

Almost half of Americans believe that recent police killings in Missouri, New York, and Maryland make up part of a broader pattern of how police deal with African Americans, according to a 2015 poll by the Public Religion Research Institute (PRRI). And while most Republicans believe these killings are isolated incidents, most Democrats and most Independents see these actions as part of a continuing pattern of abusive police behavior.

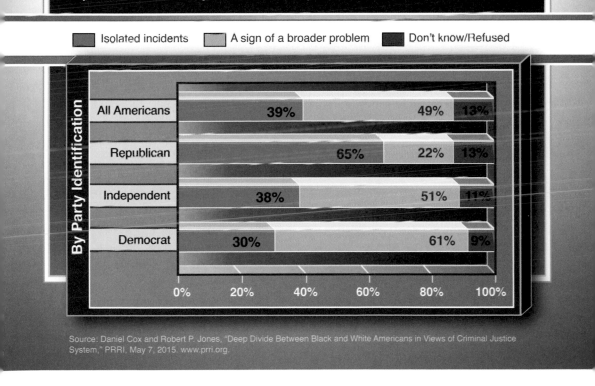

Do you think the recent killings of black men by police in Ferguson, Mo., New York City, and Baltimore are isolated incidents, or are they part of a broader pattern of how police treat black Americans?

☐ Isolated incidents   ☐ A sign of a broader problem   ☐ Don't know/Refused

By Party Identification

	Isolated incidents	A sign of a broader problem	Don't know/Refused
All Americans	39%	49%	13%
Republican	65%	22%	13%
Independent	38%	51%	11%
Democrat	30%	61%	9%

Source: Daniel Cox and Robert P. Jones, "Deep Divide Between Black and White Americans in Views of Criminal Justice System," PRRI, May 7, 2015. www.prri.org.

the conclusions made by a group of researchers who tried studying the problem of police corruption in 2016. In a report published by the US Department of Justice, researchers Philip Matthew Stinson Sr., John Liederbach, Steven P. Lab, and Steven L. Brewer Jr. investigated the nature and extent of known crimes committed by police. Because such records are not readily kept, they had to analyze news articles and court records from 2005 to 2011. They found that officers all over the United States are regularly arrested for a wide range of very serious crimes, including driving drunk, selling drugs, and committing sexual assault, robbery, and murder. "Cases in which sworn law enforcement officers act as criminals . . . strike a direct blow to the law enforcement enterprise and the essence of what it means to be a law enforcement officer: protect and serve," stated the report's authors. Moreover, their work indicates that corruption and lack of integrity are likely more widespread among police than is often thought. "Our data directly contradicts . . . the proposition that only a small group of rotten apples perpetrate the vast majority of police crime," they wrote. "Police crimes are not isolated events."[13]

Violating Civil Rights

In addition to corruption and excessive use of force, police often violate the civil rights of the citizens they have sworn to protect. One way they do this is by stopping people without probable cause. Some officers routinely stop citizens without any evidence that a crime has been committed. They may search people, or their cars, in the hope of finding evidence of some type of criminal activity. These so-called stop-and-frisk tactics are particularly common in high-crime areas where police think they have a good chance of finding criminal activity. However, it is nothing less than an abuse of power and a violation of civil rights to stop and search someone who has done nothing wrong.

Gemar Mills, the principal of Malcolm X High School in Newark, New Jersey, says the police often use stop-and-frisk techniques on his students. He argues that while the police may sometimes discover criminal activity this way, community members—particularly young people—can be significantly harmed by being the subject of police suspicion when they have done nothing wrong. "It reduces your self-confidence," he explains. "It's no different than getting robbed. Getting put up against a wall, it's no different than someone stealing your stuff. It can be traumatizing. For the police, they let you go, it's no harm, no foul. But it can make children feel the community has given up on their chance to be successful."[14]

All over the world, and even in parts of the United States, police departments manage to do their jobs well without exercising extreme force, violating citizens' rights, and engaging in corrupt and criminal behavior. As Campaign Zero puts it, "Police in England, Germany, Australia, Japan, and even cities like Buffalo, NY, and Richmond, CA, demonstrate that public safety can be ensured without killing civilians."[15] All **Americans, in every city and community, deserve the same from their officers of the law.**

US Police Do Not Abuse Their Power

"While some officers abuse their power, the majority are 'good cops.' For every officer who visits harm on someone or violates the public's trust, there are countless others who follow the rules and who want nothing more than to protect, serve and return home safe at the end of their shift."

Nick Wing, "If Most Police Officers Are 'Good Cops,' These Are Even Better," *Huffington Post*, January 13, 2015. www.huffingtonpost.com.

Consider these questions as you read:

1. Do you agree that the media exaggerates the extent of police misbehavior? Why or why not?
2. How does the perception that the American public has become better armed complicate the work that police officers do?
3. To what extent do you think police should use stop-and-frisk tactics? Should they heavily rely on them? Use them sparingly? Never use them? Explain your reasoning.

Editor's note: The discussion that follows presents common arguments made in support of this perspective, reinforced by facts, quotes, and examples taken from various sources.

In August 2016, during a preseason football game, San Francisco 49ers quarterback Colin Kaepernick sat on the bench while the national anthem played. His action was intended to protest police brutality against minorities. "I am not going to stand up to show pride in a flag for a country that oppresses black people and people of color," he said. "There are bodies in the street and people getting paid leave and getting away with murder."[16]

While some applauded Kaepernick's actions, his protest was deeply misguided and inappropriate. The reality is that most American police officers do not abuse their power. Chris Amos, a former police officer, argues that although unjustified shootings and other abuses of police power occasionally happen, they are by no means the rule. "Are there some bad apples within my profession?" asks Amos. "Absolutely and they need to be identified and fired or arrested! But . . . the vast majority do the right thing, the right way, for the right reason."[17] Amos is right. Most police officers spend their lives trying to protect people in their communities, often putting themselves in grave danger to do so. As Amos and many others point out, abuse of police power tends to be an anomaly—it simply is not a widespread problem.

The Majority of Police Officers Have Integrity

The perception that most police officers abuse their power is wildly incorrect. This harmful generalization stems from the fact that some officers do act badly, but they are in the small minority of all officers who serve their communities well. Avery Mauntel is a police officer in Las Vegas. He argues that the public tends to inflate news of bad policing and falsely assume that all police officers are corrupt. "Something bad happens halfway across the country, it still reflects poorly on us," he says. "It makes our jobs harder. [People] see something somewhere else, but that's not me. I'm not there; . . . that's not how I carry myself; that's not how I'm going to police."[18] Gene Dieppa, who served in the Miami-Dade Police Department until his retirement in 2015, agrees. "You can't blame all police [for the few bad ones]," he insists; "99 percent of police are good people and want to be your friend."[19]

> "The vast majority [of police officers] do the right thing, the right way, for the right reason."[17]
>
> —Former police officer Chris Amos

Many officers lament that the public judges all police officers on the basis of what they hear and see on the news. These media portrayals usually offer an incomplete picture of what police officers really do and focus only on problems; many reports ignore the fact that most police officers are actually doing a good job, and certainly, it does not make news when police handle a delicate or dangerous situation with skill, tact, and competence. "It sometimes feels like the only voice you ever hear is criticising you," one officer told a reporter for the *Economist*. "If you watch the TV news, our good work only gets two seconds. When we do something bad, it gets two minutes."[20]

Most Use of Force Is Justified

Criticism of police officers often centers on their use of force. However, officers legitimately do need to use force—this is a key part of their job, not an abuse of power. The use of force is a necessary response to the fact that the US population is extremely well armed. Overall, there are hundreds of millions of guns in the United States; researchers estimate that there are about the same number of guns as there are people. Officers report that they commonly face criminals with powerful weapons such as automatic guns, which can fire continuously. Force is thus the only way police officers can protect themselves, given the fact that they are confronting heavily armed criminals.

In 2016 the National Police Research Platform surveyed more than seven thousand police officers across the United States. Its results revealed an officer population that fears for its safety on a daily basis. In fact, 93 percent of respondents said that officers in their departments have become increasingly concerned about their safety. Some officers say they often worry about being hurt or killed on the job. Therefore, they often use force because they are afraid that if they do not act first, they might end up dead. D.K., an anonymous writer for the *Economist* who spoke with police officers on this topic, found that many think the proliferation of weapons among the public is making their job more difficult and dangerous. "Most of the officers I interviewed say that guns poison policing in America," says D.K. He went on to quote one of these officers as saying, "'They're literally everywhere. . . . And the problem with dealing with guns is that if I'm talking to you and you've got a gun, action always beats reaction.'"[21] Another police officer agreed, saying that officers need

Most People Believe Police Use the Right Amount of Force

Americans think that police use the right amount of force when they interact with civilians. This was the finding of a 2016 survey of more than two thousand Americans, the majority of whom said they thought police officers use appropriate amounts of force, police tactics are appropriate, and officers use deadly force only when necessary.

Most Americans Say Police Use Right Amount of Force

In general, are the tactics used by police officers too harsh, not harsh enough, or about right?

Not harsh enough
7%
Too harsh
30%
63%
About right

In general, do you think the police are too quick to use deadly force, or do they typically only use deadly force when necessary?

Too quick
42%
Only when necessary
58%

Source: Emily Ekins, "Policing in America: Understanding Public Attitudes Toward the Police. Results from a National Survey." Cato Institute, 2016. https://object.cato.org.

to take action against heavily armed criminals rather than waiting to react; "If I take a punch and I'm knocked out, they could take my gun."[22] This is why she and other officers believe they need to stay ahead of such threats by using higher levels of force.

While there is limited data on the matter, the statistics that do exist indicate that it is rare for an officer to hurt, let alone kill, a member of the community. In fact, the number of people harmed by police officers is very small compared to the total number of people who are in contact with them every day. There are no official statistics on fatal uses of force, but a 2015 Bureau of Justice Statistics report confirms that nonfatal force—which includes shouting, pushing, hitting, or pointing a gun—is rare. It found that between 2002 and 2011, approximately 44 million US residents aged sixteen or older had face-to-face contact with the police. Only 1.6 percent of them were subject to the use of nonfatal force by the police.

Police Behave Appropriately

Police have also been unfairly demonized for using stop-and-frisk tactics, which help police catch criminals in the act. This practice allows police in high-crime neighborhoods to stop people and search them when they have reason to suspect criminal activity. While critics charge that it is an abuse of power, both police officers and criminologists maintain that this practice is constitutional and is extremely effective for reducing crime. When people know that police are aggressively enforcing the law, they are less likely to break it. Stop-and-frisk tactics have been widely used in New York City, where they have helped significantly decrease crime. Former New York City mayor Rudolph W. Giuliani, who championed such tactics, reports that between 1994 and 2013, stop and frisk was responsible for an 85 percent reduction in crime. "This practice dramatically reduced the number of guns, knives and other dangerous weapons, as well as illicit drugs, in the city,"[23] he argues.

"In the overwhelming majority of cases it is not the cops, but the people they stop, who can prevent detentions from turning into tragedies."[24]

—Sunil Dutta, a veteran police officer in Los Angeles

In cases where police and civilians violently interact, the real cause is rarely an officer's abuse of power; rather, it is a lack of respect from community members. Police officers report that situations can violently escalate should members of the public challenge them or fail to comply with their orders. According to Sunil Dutta, a seventeen-year-veteran police officer in Los Angeles, police officers never intend to hurt or kill people. "Cops are not murderers. No officer goes out in the field wishing to shoot anyone, armed or unarmed," he insists. "In the overwhelming majority of cases it is not the cops, but the people they stop, who can prevent detentions from turning into tragedies." He advises, "Do what the officer tells you to and it will end safely for both of you."[24] Indeed, citizens need to respect and obey police officers so that officers can do their jobs effectively.

Dutta, Dieppa, Mauntel, and Amos are among the tens of thousands of police officers who use their power responsibly and appropriately. The high-quality work they do each day to keep America's towns and cities safe is proof that abuse of police power is not a widespread problem in the United States.

Chapter Two

Are Police Biased Against Racial Minorities?

Police Are Biased Against Racial Minorities

- Research and personal stories reveal that racial bias against minorities is extremely common.
- US police officers routinely use racial profiling.
- The United States has few laws to prevent racial profiling.
- A lack of diversity in police departments contributes to racial bias.

The Debate at a Glance

Police Are Not Biased Against Racial Minorities

- There is no evidence that racial bias is a serious problem.
- Police use criminal profiling, not racial profiling.
- Minorities are targeted by the police because they are statistically more likely to commit a crime.
- Diversity in police departments does not prevent racial bias.

Police Are Biased Against Racial Minorities

"Minorities, particularly African Americans, are subjected to a disproportionate level of police interventions like traffic stops, searches, arrests and the use of deadly force."

Ivan Yihshyan Sun, "Other Real Factors Can Obscure the Role in Racism in Policing," *New York Times*, November 25, 2014. www.nytimes.com.

Consider these questions as you read:

1. Do you think that stories about racial bias from citizens prove that racial bias is a serious problem in American police departments? Why or why not?
2. Do you think laws should prevent police from using racial profiling to target suspected criminals? Or it a useful policing technique? Explain your reasoning.
3. How does the racial composition of police departments contribute to racial tensions between police and the populations they serve?

Editor's note: The discussion that follows presents common arguments made in support of this perspective, reinforced by facts, quotes, and examples taken from various sources.

Shanel Berry has two sons—fifteen-year-old Dallas and eleven-year-old Amari. Berry has taught her children to be proud, confident, and vocal about their opinions. She has raised them to stand up for what they believe in and for what is right. However, Berry and her sons are African American, and there is one occasion on which she tells her sons to exhibit none of these qualities—in the event they are stopped by police. "In that case," write reporters Jack Healy and Nikole Hannah-Jones, "she wants her sons to be cautious and just obey any orders the police may give them—even

Ferguson Police Intentionally Discriminate Against African Americans

After the 2014 shooting of Michael Brown in Ferguson, Missouri, the Department of Justice (DOJ) investigated the issue of racial bias and police officers there. The findings showed that African Americans in Ferguson are far more likely than whites to be stopped, arrested, and charged with crimes. For instance, although African Americans made up only 67 percent of Ferguson's population between 2012 and 2014, they accounted for 90 percent or more of vehicle stops, citations, and arrests during that period. The DOJ concluded, "Ferguson's approach to law enforcement both reflects and reinforces racial bias, including stereotyping." Although the DOJ report did not address police-minority relations in other cities, it is likely that such practices and attitudes exist in other US cities.

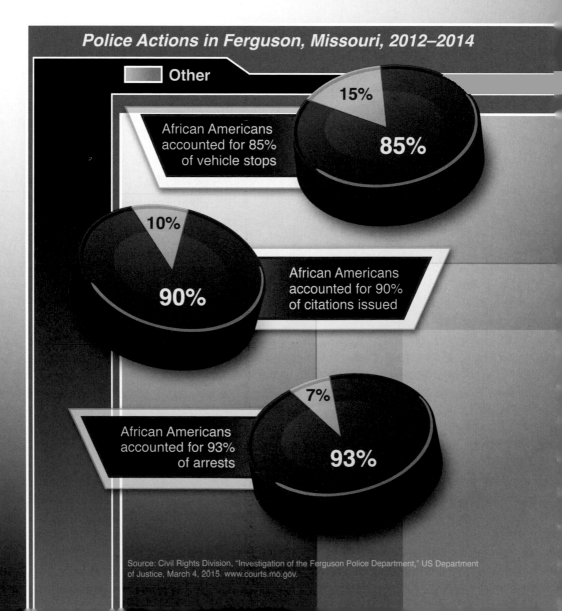

Police Actions in Ferguson, Missouri, 2012–2014

Other

15%

African Americans accounted for 85% of vehicle stops

85%

10%

African Americans accounted for 90% of citations issued

90%

7%

African Americans accounted for 93% of arrests

93%

Source: Civil Rights Division, "Investigation of the Ferguson Police Department," US Department of Justice, March 4, 2015. www.courts.mo.gov.

if they feel they were stopped for no reason."[25] Berry is afraid that if her children are not quiet and compliant should they encounter the police, they risk being hurt—or even killed. She is not the only African American parent who gives her children this advice; thousands of others believe that police officers treat minorities less fairly than whites and are more likely to use deadly force against them. Unfortunately, these fears are justified: there is widespread evidence that American police officers are racially biased.

Racial Bias Is Pervasive

Numerous studies show that the police arrest minorities and use force against them at far higher rates than whites. For example, in 2015 the US Department of Justice issued a report on the Ferguson Police Department that revealed pronounced racial bias against African Americans in that Missouri city. Researchers found that while African Americans make up 67 percent of Ferguson's population, they account for 85 percent of vehicle stops, 90 percent of citations, and 93 percent of arrests. African Americans were also more likely than whites to be searched during vehicle stops, even though they were actually less likely to be found with contraband. Finally, almost 90 percent of the documented cases of force that occurred in Ferguson during the time period that was studied were against African Americans.

Another study on racial bias was conducted by the *New York Times* and found similar results. According to a report on the results of the study, an analysis of traffic stops and arrest data from Greensboro, North Carolina, showed significant differences in how people were treated based on their race. "Officers pulled over African American drivers for traffic violations at a rate far out of proportion with their share of the local driving population," note the authors of the report. "They used their discretion to search black drivers or their cars more than twice as often as white motorists—even though they found drugs and weapons significantly more often when the driver was white. Officers were more likely to stop black drivers for no discernible reason."[26] Police officers were also more likely to use force against African American drivers, even if they put up no physical resistance.

Personal stories support these findings. For example, Holly, an African American woman who lives in Ferguson, spoke with a researcher at Human Rights Watch about her experiences with racial bias. "They'll stop them just for being black," Holly says of the Ferguson police. "I've actually stood there and watched cousins of mine get pulled over. [The police] would sit them down, pat them down, even after they knew they had the wrong person. I have so many of those stories."[27] Surveys have yielded evidence of such stories all over the country. For example, the Cato Institute, in collaboration with YouGov, surveyed thousands of people in 2015 and 2016 and found that African Americans are almost twice as likely as whites to say that a police officer has used abusive language or profanity toward them and that they know someone who has been physically mistreated by the police.

Racial Profiling Is Pronounced

African Americans and other minorities are also the victims of racial profiling, which is when police officers target people for investigation on the basis of their race. Evidence suggests racial profiling is very common in the United States. According to the American Civil Liberties Union, "It occurs every day, in cities and towns across the country, when law enforcement and private security target people of color for humiliating and often frightening detentions, interrogations, and searches without evidence of criminal activity and based on perceived race, ethnicity, national origin, or religion."[28] In the Cato/YouGov study, almost two-thirds of those surveyed believe that the police use racial profiling to decide which motorists and pedestrians to stop. The majority of respondents also said they are opposed to this practice.

> "They'll stop them just for being black. . . . I've actually stood there and watched cousins of mine get pulled over."[27]
>
> —Holly, an African American woman who lives in Ferguson, Missouri

Kiairus Diamond and Joshua Rodriguez, students in Newark, New Jersey, have experienced racial profiling firsthand. Kiairus is a sophomore in high school, and his friend Joshua is a junior. They say they are often subject to racial profiling by the police and have been searched multiple times, despite the fact that they have done nothing wrong. The students talked with journalist Daniel Bergner about their experiences. Bergner writes, "'Cops in Newark,' Kiairus said, 'if your skin is like this'—he touched his dark forearm—'they're going to think you're on your way to doing something, or coming from doing something.'"[29]

A Critical Lack of Laws

While the existence of racial profiling is widely recognized and its harms are frequently acknowledged, there has been no effective action to stop this practice. According to a 2014 report by the National Association for the Advancement of Colored People (NAACP), the United States simply does not have any laws that adequately address racial profiling. "The current status of laws across the fifty states leaves little hope for a meaningful solution to this problem," notes the NAACP. "Currently, 30 states in the country have one or more anti-racial profiling law on the books. However, not one adequately meets all the provisions required for an effective law, making them inadequate tools to significantly curb the practice of racial profiling."[30] Without effective laws to stop it, racial profiling will continue.

Make Police Departments More Diverse

One reason why racial profiling is so common is that most police forces are very homogenous. In many departments, the majority of officers are white. Ronald Weitzer, a professor of sociology at George Washington University, polled almost two thousand Americans and found that more than 70 percent of African Americans, Hispanics, and whites feel that a police department should have a similar racial composition to the city it serves. Weitzer says that diversity can significantly improve the relationship between the police and the community, and many communities recognize this and want racially diverse police forces. "Diversity can help to build trust and confidence in the police: the more a police department reflects the composition of the local population, the higher the department's reputation among residents, which can provide a foundation to build further trust, coupled with other needed reforms,"[31] he says.

Michael Dieppa agrees that it is important to have a police department that represents community demographics. Dieppa is head of the Miami-Dade Public Safety Training Institute and is tasked with hiring new officers. "Every time we put a class into the academy in Miami, I looked at the demographics and made sure we'd put in a number of people equivalent to the demographics of our community," he says. "If we were 60 percent Hispanic, we were going to get 25 to 30 Hispanics. If we were 20 percent black, we were going to put in 10 to 15 black officers."[32] As a result of such careful selection, he believes that Miami avoids some of the policing problems that other communities have.

"Diversity can help to build trust and confidence in the police."[31]

—Ronald Weitzer, a professor of sociology at George Washington University in Washington, DC

Unfortunately, carefully curated police departments like the one in Miami-Dade County are rare in the United States. Throughout most of the country, racial profiling and racial bias are very common and result in the unfair treatment of minorities, particularly African Americans.

Police Are Not Biased Against Racial Minorities

"The default position has become that, whenever police resort to deadly force, they are wrong—and racially motivated. This despite the fact that, in many cases, both the officers and the subjects are black, and in many cases, the shootings turn out to be fully justified or sometimes just tragic errors."

Deborah Daniels, "Police Are Pulling Back When We Need Them Most," *Indianapolis Business Journal*, September 10, 2016. www.ibj.com.

Consider these questions as you read:

1. In your opinion, has the extent of racial bias among police been exaggerated? How should the lack of research on this topic be interpreted?
2. How strong is the argument that police officers use criminal profiling, not racial profiling, to do their work?
3. What are some advantages of having a racially diverse police department? In what ways might diverse police departments not matter?

Editor's note: The discussion that follows presents common arguments made in support of this perspective, reinforced by facts, quotes, and examples taken from various sources.

US police officers are often accused of being racially biased; critics say they unfairly target African Americans and other minorities on the basis of race rather than on evidence of criminal activity. However, criminal data reveals that focusing on race is not an expression of racism but rather a sound policing strategy. When police focus on minorities, they are not doing so out of racial bias but because they have evidence that some minority groups are more likely to be involved in criminal activity. In reality, bias against racial minorities is uncommon in the United States.

Minorities are Disproportionally Involved in Crime

Data suggests that compared to the general population, young African Americans are much more likely to be involved in crime. This is what economics professor Walter Williams found when he examined the Uniform Crime Reporting statistics, an official collection of data on crime published by the FBI. The data revealed that young African Americans commit a disproportionally high percentage of criminal activity, compared to the general population. "According to the Uniform Crime Report for 2009, among people 18 or younger, blacks were charged with 58 percent of murder and non-negligent manslaughter, 67 percent of robberies, 42 percent of aggravated assaults and 43 percent of auto thefts,"[33] says Williams. Given that African Americans make up only about 13 percent of the population, his analysis is but one example that disproves the claim that police act unfairly toward minorities.

The Problem of Racial Bias Has Been Exaggerated

While some individual officers might be racially biased, there is no evidence that bias against minorities is a widespread or institutionalized problem. This is because there are no studies or statistical data showing that racial bias is common. Instead, most charges of racial bias stem from anecdotal evidence or personal opinion.

Former FBI director James B. Comey has suggested that many Americans protest racial bias without knowing the facts. "People of good will are protesting . . . because they believe there is an epidemic of police violence against black people," he says. "Of course, however good their hearts, however good their intentions, Americans actually have no idea whether the number of black people or brown people or white people being shot by police is up, down, or sideways over the last 10 years. They have no idea whether black people or brown people are more likely to be shot during encounters than white people are."[34] Overall, the vast majority of police officers are not acting out of bias. Rather they are simply trying to help prevent crime in America's communities, regardless of what race community members and criminals may be.

Moreover, only a minority of African Americans say that police have recently treated them unfairly because of their race. This was the finding of a 2015 survey by the Gallup organization. Researchers asked whether respondents could think of any occasion in the past thirty days when the police had treated them unfairly because of their race. Just 18 percent responded "yes." Interestingly, the percentage of African Americans who say they have been treated unfairly by police because of their race has actually decreased in the past ten years. When Gallup asked the same question in 2004, 25 percent of those polled answered "yes." Surveys like these show that although racial discrimination does happen, the problem is not as widespread as many claim it is.

> "However good their hearts, however good their intentions, Americans actually have no idea whether the number of black people or brown people or white people being shot by police is up, down, or sideways over the last 10 years."[34]
>
> —James B. Comey, the former director of the FBI

The Relationship Between Race and Police Arrests

Sometimes officers do base their decisions on race, but this does not stem from racism. Rather, they target certain groups of people and certain neighborhoods based on the levels of crime that have existed among these groups and areas in the past. "There is no racial profiling. There just isn't," explains Steve James, president of the Long Beach Police Officers Association in California. James says "there is criminal profiling,"[35] which is a police strategy that involves targeting certain groups of people based on the likelihood that they will commit a crime. Minority groups are statistically more likely to live in areas with higher crime, which means they more often interact with or are sought by police. However, this is more a matter of demographics and less a matter of racism.

While some racial tension in law enforcement is inevitable, it is important to realize that when police focus on minorities, it is usually because minority populations tend to have higher crime rates. An analysis by Alfred Blumstein, a professor at Carnegie Mellon University in

The Majority of African Americans Feel That Police Treat Them Fairly

Gallup surveys conducted between 1997 and 2015 reveal that the majority of African Americans polled think the police treat them fairly. Respondents were asked if they had, in the last month, been treated less fairly by the police because they were black. The majority answered no, indicating that no widespread racial bias exists among police officers.

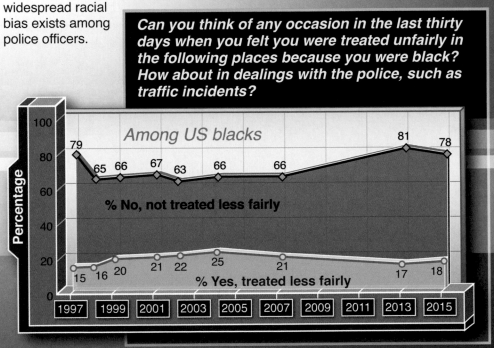

Can you think of any occasion in the last thirty days when you felt you were treated unfairly in the following places because you were black? How about in dealings with the police, such as traffic incidents?

Among US blacks

% No, not treated less fairly

% Yes, treated less fairly

Source: Frank Newport, "Despite Unrest, Blacks Do Not Feel More Mistreated by Police," Gallup, August 3, 2015. www.gallup.com.

Pennsylvania, shows that minorities are statistically much more likely to be involved in serious crimes. Blumstein looked at the FBI's Uniform Crime Reporting statistics and found that compared to whites, the per capita arrest rate for African Americans is 7.3 times higher for robbery and 5.9 times higher for murder. These higher crime rates mean that police spend more time patrolling minority communities, which increases the risk of conflict between officers and community members. As Blumstein explains, "Those crime differences lead to more intensive police attention and patrol presence in the poorer minority communities, increasing the possibility of excessive responses or even reasonable responses being interpreted as excessive."[36]

Increasing Diversity Is Not a Solution

When conflict does occur between police and minorities, some have suggested it be addressed by making police departments more diverse. In reality, however, making police departments more diverse has no bearing on racial bias or on conflict between police and minorities. This is because of how the police force has historically been used in the United States. Jamelle Bouie is the chief political correspondent for *Slate* magazine. He argues that the relationship between US police and minorities will never be perfect because of the fact that, historically, the police were often used to control minorities. "The earliest police antecedents were slave patrols and anti-native militias, built to suppress rebellion and combat Native Americans," he explains. "After the Civil War, Southern whites used police as a new tool for control, terrorizing blacks under the guise of law enforcement, from lynchings—often organized or supported by local sheriffs—to convict leasing [using convicts for labor]."[37] Even though this is no longer the case, this history will forever stain the relationship between police officers and minorities, no matter the racial makeup of a police department.

Moreover, research suggests that diverse police departments do little to lessen conflict between police and minorities. One such study was conducted by Brad Smith, a researcher from Wayne State University in Detroit. He looked at how officer-involved homicides relate to police diversity and found that regardless of the diversity of a police force, cities with more African Americans are more likely to experience more police shootings. In other words, diversity did not

> "Police will always be seen as representatives of the larger establishment. As such, tensions between police and citizens may be a function of the police role."[38]
>
> —Brad Smith, a researcher from Wayne State University in Detroit

significantly reduce the number of people killed by police; this number was driven more by population demographics than police department demographics. "Regardless of who is carrying out the police function," says Smith, "police will always be seen as representatives of the larger establishment. As such, tensions between police and citizens may be a function of the police role."[38] This appears to be true in the city of Baltimore, which has a fairly diverse police force. Journalist Jen Fifield reports that 42 percent of the police department is black compared to 63 percent of the city's population. Despite this diversity, Baltimore has experienced widespread conflict between African Americans and the police, and there is evidence that the police stop, search, and arrest African Americans at higher rates than the rest of the population.

While conflict between minorities and police officers in the United States exists, most charges of racial bias are not backed by evidence. In reality, bias against racial minorities is not a serious problem in the United States.

Chapter Three

Can Technology and Training Help Police Officers Do Their Jobs Better?

Technology and Training Can Help Police Officers Do Their Jobs Better

- Body cameras encourage both police and citizens to behave better.
- Demilitarizing the police will improve relationships with the community and reduce violence.
- Training officers in de-escalation techniques can reduce their use of force.
- Racial bias training reduces conflict between the police and minorities by making police more sensitive to cultural differences.

The Debate at a Glance

Proposed Technology and Police Training Are Ineffective

- Body cameras give police officers and police departments even more power.
- Police body cameras threaten civil liberties.
- Preventing police departments from receiving surplus military equipment impedes their ability to do good work.
- It is impossible to eliminate racial bias through training because of the way bias is embedded in the mind.

Technology and Training Can Help Police Officers Do Their Jobs Better

"States should update and intensify training for law enforcement personnel on community relations, biased policing, and de-escalation of violence techniques."

Antonio M. Ginatta, "A Call for Police Accountability," *Hill*, September 30, 2014. http://thehill.com.

Consider these questions as you read:

1. What effect do you think body cameras have on police behavior? What about on the behavior of citizens?
2. Do you think it is inappropriate for police officers to act like soldiers and be equipped with military gear? Why or why not?
3. What effect do you think racial bias training might have on encounters between police and civilians? Explain your answer.

Editor's note: The discussion that follows presents common arguments made in support of this perspective, reinforced by facts, quotes, and examples taken from various sources.

In February 2012 the police department in Rialto, California, began a yearlong experiment to investigate what happens when police officers wear body cameras. In half of all the shifts that officers were assigned to, they were required to wear body cameras, and for the other half of the shifts the officers did not wear cameras. Researchers then tallied all of the incidents in which any officer used force, and they tracked formal complaints against the officers. The researchers found that when officers wore cameras, their job performance significantly improved. Their use of force was reduced by more than 50 percent, and formal complaints decreased considerably (nearly ten times less than what they had been in the twelve months prior to body camera use). Experiments like this prove what seems intuitively true: technology and training can considerably improve the way police officers do their jobs.

Body Cameras Increase Accountability

A body camera is a highly effective tool for improving police performance. When cameras are recording their actions, both police officers and members of the community are likely to think more carefully about their behavior and treat each other more respectfully. As a result, encounters are less likely to end in conflict or violence. "When you know you're being watched you behave a little better," Rialto police chief Tony Farrar explains. "That's just human nature. . . . As an officer you act a bit more professional, follow the rules a bit better."[39] The same is true of members of the public, who tend to be more polite to officers when they know they are on camera.

Cameras also help prevent abuses of power by the police. They tell the whole, true story in the event a police officer is unable or unwilling to do so. In legal disputes regarding interactions between police officers and citizens, courts tend to side with the police. This means it can be easy for officers to lie about what happened. Matthew Segal, legal director of the American Civil Liberties Union of Massachusetts, says body cameras help keep officers honest and therefore help protect the public. "When video is absent, court proceedings can too often disadvantage civilians, whose claims can so easily be disbelieved when they contradict [an] officer's account,"[40] he says. Body cameras help prevent abuse because they show exactly what happened.

> "When you know you're being watched you behave a little better. That's just human nature."[39]
>
> —Tony Farrar, the police chief of Rialto, California

In some cities, the use of body cameras has noticeably improved police behavior. Consider what happened when the New Orleans Police Department started to use body cameras in 2014. "They can't get away with some of the practices they used to," says Danny Engelberg, chief of trials for the Orleans Public Defenders office. "Busting into people's houses, going into people's cars, just coming up to people and searching them with impunity. . . . We just aren't seeing as much of that."[41]

Demilitarize the Police

While adding tools like body cameras can help decrease tension between police and civilians, taking away other technology and tools can also improve relations. Consider that in recent years police departments have been equipped with large amounts of surplus military gear, such as guns and armored vehicles, in the hopes that this equipment will help them do their jobs better. However, this type of equipment makes the police function more like a military and encourages community members and police officers to see each other as opponents in a war rather than as partners in a community. This militarization of the police makes conflict between the two groups much more likely.

Thus, police departments should be demilitarized where possible. Police officers have a completely different role than soldiers; they should not act like soldiers, and they should not have such weaponry. "Although police officers wear uniforms and carry weapons, the similarity ends there," notes Susan Rahr, director of Washington State's police academy. "The missions and rules of engagement are completely different. The soldier's mission is that of a warrior: to conquer. . . . The police officer's mission is that of a guardian: to protect. . . . Soldiers come into communities as an outside, occupying force. Guardians are members of the community, protecting from within."[42]

Arming police officers as if they were soldiers increases the chance that interactions with the community will end in violence or death. An example of how this is possible comes from Habersham County, Georgia, in 2014. During a special weapons and tactics (SWAT) team raid on the home of a suspected drug dealer, police threw a flash-bang grenade—a device that is designed to cause a loud bang and a flash of light to temporarily disorient an enemy—into the house. The grenade landed in the playpen of a one-year-old boy and exploded on his pillow. The boy was seriously injured and spent weeks in the hospital burn unit. The infant

Body Cameras Can Improve Police Behavior

Outfitting police with body cameras can both reduce their use of force and the number of complaints they receive from the public. This was the finding of a year-long study conducted by researchers in the Southern California city of Rialto. The study compared three years of data about use of force and public complaints to one experimental year in which officers wore body cameras (2012–2013). Researchers found that during the year body cameras were worn, officers used less force against citizens and also received fewer complaints about their behavior. The study concluded that body cameras can have significant effects on the nature of police work.

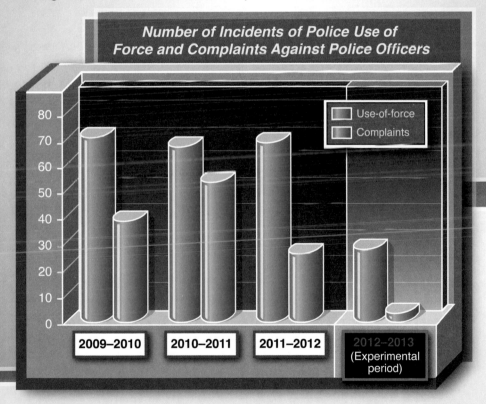

Number of Incidents of Police Use of Force and Complaints Against Police Officers

Source: Matthew Feeney, "Watching the Watchmen: Best Practices for Body Cameras," *CATO Policy Analysis*, October 27, 2015. https://www.cato.org.

was innocent, and surely the suspected drug dealer could have been apprehended in another manner. This tragedy could have been avoided had police not been armed with military weapons.

Focus on De-escalation

Police officers also need to be trained to de-escalate situations, which means backing off from conflict rather than amping tensions up or resorting to force. Many law enforcement situations can actually be resolved without force. Officers can calm suspects down by simply speaking with them rather than by physically subduing them. According to Rahr, force is often the wrong approach: "When you approach a situation like RoboCop, you're going to create hostility that wasn't there before."[43] Instead, Rahr and others advise that officers be trained in how to talk to people and resolve conflicts. Officers can also learn to work together to de-escalate a situation—for example, in a situation where one officer is afraid or angry, and thus likely to resort to violence, the other officer can step in and calm things down. According to Chuck Wexler of the Police Executive Research Forum, such techniques are extremely effective. "How many cases would have been prevented when someone is obviously getting upset and losing their cool, if another officer had said, 'Hey, step back, let me take over?'" he says. "That's what you need—cool heads to prevail."[44]

> "When you approach a situation like RoboCop, you're going to create hostility that wasn't there before."[43]
>
> —Susan Rahr, director of Washington State's police academy

Many police officers admit that they use force because they are afraid of being harmed themselves. However, there is strong evidence that police officers need not be so fearful. According to law professor and former police officer Seth Stoughton, violent attacks on police officers are statistically quite rare, especially when one considers that police officers have about 63 million interactions with civilians every year. "In percentage terms," says Stoughton, "officers were assaulted in about 0.09 percent of all interactions, were injured in some way in 0.02 percent of interactions, and were feloniously killed in 0.00008 percent of interactions."[45] In light of such statistics, police officers would do well to keep the risks they face in perspective and realize it is not always necessary to react with force.

Racial Bias Training

Another reason why police tend to use more force than necessary is that many have racial biases that affect the way they interpret and react to the people they encounter. Researchers have found that it is common for all people to have racial biases, even when they think that they do not. To reduce the harms that result from racial bias, police officers should be trained in cultural responsiveness. Such training can help them become aware of cultural differences and recognize that racial biases and other prejudices exist. This, in turn, will help them better understand the people they encounter, treat them more fairly, and build mutual trust and respect. This is one of the many ways that training can help police do their jobs more effectively.

Proposed Technology and Police Training Are Ineffective

"Rather than developing new tools, extending training, or collecting more data in hopes of improving how policing happens, our best work may be to imagine how we can shrink the size and scope of police forces . . . [and try to] to mitigate and reduce the harms we do to each other without law enforcement intervention."

Rachel Herzing, "Let's Reduce, Not Reform, Policing in America," Open Society Foundations, October 6, 2016. www.opensocietyfoundations.org.

Consider these questions as you read:

1. What threats might body cameras pose to the public?
2. When might police officers need military equipment? Are these weapons justified, in your opinion? Explain your reasoning.
3. In your opinion, should police officers undergo racial bias training? What are the benefits? What are the drawbacks?

Editor's note: The discussion that follows presents common arguments made in support of this perspective, reinforced by facts, quotes, and examples taken from various sources.

An abundance of hopeful proposals exist to improve policing; these include everything from using technology to record police stops to training police to tap into their racial biases. While many of these ideas are well-intentioned, little evidence shows that they actually work.

Likewise, not much hard data exists about what actually helps police do their jobs better. Wesley G. Skogan, Maarten Van Craen, and Cari Hennessy should know—they authored a 2014 research study about the topic. "We know virtually nothing about the short- or long-term effects associated with police training of any type,"[46] they concluded. Former police officer Dave Klinger agrees. As a result of this lack of scientific knowledge, he says, in some areas of policing "we're flying by the seat of our pants."[47] Overall, there is no evidence that training or technology can effectively reduce abuse of police power. In fact, some of these proposals even pose a threat to society.

Body Cameras Do Not Prevent Abuse

While police departments across the country have embraced the use of body cameras, the reality is that cameras can do little to reduce abuses of police power. Police departments often control these cameras and the footage obtained from them and use the cameras in ways that benefit the police rather than the community. In controversial situations, body camera footage is often released only when it proves the police version of what happened. This is why Robinson Meyer, an associate editor at the *Atlantic* magazine, argues that body camera footage ends up serving a police narrative. "Instead of making officers more accountable and transparent to the public, body cameras may be making officers and departments more powerful than they were before."[48] Many states have actually passed laws that prevent the public from having access to such footage. This means that rather than providing an impartial record of what happened, body cameras end up supporting the police version of events. Notes *Huffington Post* reporter Andy Campbell, "It's nearly impossible to find a case in which a body camera law is passed unconditionally, footage is released in a timely manner, and officers, departments or lawmakers don't stand in the way of due process."[49]

Not only do body cameras fail to protect ordinary citizens, but these

"Instead of making officers more accountable and transparent to the public, body cameras may be making officers and departments more powerful than they were before."[48]

—Robinson Meyer, an associate editor at the *Atlantic*

Mandatory Diversity Training Does Not Eliminate Racial Bias

Calls for diversity training to eliminate racial bias among police are misguided. Mandatory training and other forced efforts to reduce bias in the corporate world have actually had the opposite effect, according to research published in 2016. Companies that have instituted mandatory diversity training to reduce workplace bias, hiring tests to limit recruitment bias, and employee grievance systems for reporting problem managers have not eliminated bias. In fact, companies that have forced these programs on their workforces seem to be experiencing *more* bias and *less* diversity—and there is no reason to believe that the outcome would be any different for police departments.

Percent change over five years in diversity among managers

Type of program	White		Black		Hispanic		Asian	
	Men	Women	Men	Women	Men	Women	Men	Women
Mandatory diversity training				-9.2			-4.5	-5.4
Hiring tests		-3.8	-10.2	-9.1	-6.7	-8.8		-9.3
Grievance systems		-2.7	-7.3	-4.8		-4.7	-11.3	-4.1

Source: Frank Dobbin and Alexandra Kalev, "Why Diversity Programs Fail," *Harvard Business Review*, July/August 2016. https://hbr.org.

cameras actually pose a threat to civil liberties. When police wear body cameras, the devices record everything that happens in front of them. This is a serious threat to the privacy of both criminals and law-abiding citizens, who may have difficult, private, and even embarrassing moments of their lives recorded and potentially shared without their knowledge or consent. This is why **Matthew** Feeney, a policy analyst at the Cato Institute, says, "There are privacy concerns for persons who do not want their police encounters on the evening news or splashed across social media."[50]

Demilitarizing Police Is Not a Solution

Another equipment-related suggestion to reduce the abuse of police power is to decrease departments' access to heavy military-style weapons; this will supposedly reduce their ability to inflict damage on citizens. However, forcing police to give up their equipment would actually have very negative consequences. Police officers frequently face criminals who are heavily armed, and they need heavy equipment to appropriately respond. Charles "Sid" Heal, a retired commander of the Special Enforcement Bureau of the Los Angeles County Sheriff's Department, is among many who think that taking weapons away from police serves only to give criminals the upper hand. "Criminals and terrorists have increasingly equipped themselves with high-powered weapons, explosive devices and protective armor," he says. As such, they "enjoy the advantages provided by choosing the time, location and circumstances for their nefarious activities." Heal and others insist that police departments should not be the ones to disarm. Rather, the government should spend its energy making sure that such weapons do not fall into the hands of criminals and terrorists. "Complaints that [police weapons] are too 'militaristic' . . . is like complaining a welder's helmet is ugly," says Heal. "All workers are entitled to the tools and protective gear needed for the hazards they confront."[51]

Cases in which military equipment was improperly used are very rare; in most cases, police use their equipment responsibly. "Law enforcement all over the country has a hard job to do," says Pentagon press secretary John Kirby; "99 percent of them all do it very well. And some of the [military-style] equipment that they get through [the Department of Defense] helps them do that job."[52] Sheriff Larry Amerson of Calhoun County, Alabama, agrees. "Take [equipment] away from anyone who used [it] improperly, absolutely, but don't punish everyone." He explains that if such equipment were taken away from his department, officers would not be equipped to deal with the serious threats they face every day. "If we have an active shooter situation with an armed person," Amerson worries that his officers won't "have any piece of equipment to move in"[53] to protect the officers or the community members they are there to serve.

Training Will Not Eliminate Racial Bias

Finally, training has been proposed to eliminate officers' alleged racial bias, which many claim fuels problematic interactions between police and civilians. In reality, however, training will not eliminate racial bias. Racial bias is buried deep within the mind; it influences people's actions without their even being aware of it. As a result, it is extremely difficult to eliminate, and certainly it will not be eradicated via a few hours of seminars. "Studies have shown that when someone's own implicit bias is 'exposed' by disclosing it to her, that person will correct her own explicit judgments in follow-up trials," explains Josh Green, a political science professor. "But is this correction actually changing anything deep within the brain that forms the foundation of this implicit bias? Probably not." As a result, Green and others have serious doubts about the extent to which training can have any impact on officers' deep-seated perspectives and tendencies. "More racial sensitivity training for police officers can't hurt, but we shouldn't think that it's a cure-all for implicit racial bias,"[54] Green says.

> "More racial sensitivity training for police officers can't hurt, but we shouldn't think that it's a cure-all for implicit racial bias."[54]
>
> —Josh Green, a political science professor at Ohlone College in Fremont, California

Green is not alone in his assessment that training will do little to improve police interactions with the public. University of Colorado professor Joshua Correll specializes in the study of bias. He says that although bias can be changed in a controlled setting such as a laboratory, it can quickly return once a person leaves that setting. "Just as [biases] can be changed or temporarily erased in the lab, they can be rebuilt in society, in a real world that rebuilds stereotypical affiliations," he says. "And guess what? The bias comes back, like they were never touched."[55]

While training and technology may seem an easy fix to mend the relationship between police and the public, none of the current proposals aimed at doing so will be effective. Some may actually harm society. For all of these reasons, such proposals should be abandoned.

Chapter Four

Should US Police Departments Be Reformed?

Policing Reforms Are Needed

- The police should be put under federal control.
- Police need to be trained on how to build better relationships with communities.
- Officers should be trained to use force only in extreme situations.
- US police officers should be held more accountable for misbehavior.

The Debate at a Glance

Policing Reforms Are Not Needed

- Federalizing control over the police could encourage corruption and abuse of power.
- Good community relationships do not prevent conflict between the police and the community.
- Broken-windows policing should be retained because it helps prevent major crimes.

Policing Reforms Are Needed

"Policing is broken. . . . We've got to find a way to build trust [between the police and the community]."

—Former police chief Norm Stamper

Quoted in Michel Martin, "Former Police Chief Has a Plan for 'How to Fix America's Police,'" NPR, July 10, 2016. www.npr.org.

Consider these questions as you read:

1. What effect would putting police departments under federal control have, in your opinion?
2. How do good relationships with communities help police officers do their jobs better?
3. Do you think the threat to police officers is exaggerated by department training? Why or why not?

Editor's note: The discussion that follows presents common arguments made in support of this perspective, reinforced by facts, quotes, and examples from various sources.

In recent years there has been substantial criticism of police in the United States. Publicized shootings have even provoked widespread public protests and riots, with protesters complaining about the way police approach their work. It is clear that the relationship between police and the communities they serve needs improvement. The most effective way to change police behavior is to reform the departments that train and manage them.

The Federal Government Should Have Control over the Police

The first major change to make involves who controls the police. Currently, there are a multitude of individual police departments, and each has a different way of operating and training officers. Control over police should therefore be transferred to the federal government so that training and protocols can be standardized.

Rosa Brooks, a former senior adviser at the US State Department, acknowledges that the current system does not work well. "The United States has a patchwork of law enforcement agencies, including some 18,000 separate state and local police departments and 73 federal law enforcement agencies," she explains. "The 18,000 departments include town and city police, state police, sheriff's offices, university police, transport system police, and a range of other 'special jurisdiction' departments [that] have nearly as many different recruitment policies, training programs, disciplinary policies, equipment and weapons policies, and standard operating procedures."[56] The US police system is so fragmented that it cannot even be said that the country has a police force; rather, it has multiple forces, which accounts for the disparity in police procedure and behavior.

This lack of centralization and cooperation means that departments often operate inefficiently and chaotically. There is a lack of knowledge about what police are doing, and thus it is extremely difficult to identify and institute reforms. Author Daniel Lazare thinks that placing police departments under a centralized authority like the federal government could make police operate more efficiently. "Does America really need 18,000 police departments?" he asks. "Couldn't the same tasks be conducted more efficiently and fairly if the departments were consolidated and placed firmly under federal control?" Lazare points out that other countries have consolidated the control of their police departments with great success. Such countries experience lower levels of police brutality and other problems because they are better able to monitor and control what the police are doing. "Where Britain's police forces are firmly under the control of the Home

> "Does America really need 18,000 police departments? Couldn't the same tasks be conducted more efficiently and fairly if the departments were consolidated and placed firmly under federal control?"[57]
>
> —Daniel Lazare, author of *The Frozen Republic: How the Constitution Is Paralyzing Democracy*

Office while France's are under the Ministry of the Interior . . . America's are virtually autonomous," says Lazare. "Absence of knowledge means an absence of control, which means that local departments behave with relative impunity."[57]

Improve Relationships

Police departments also need to train officers to have better relationships with the communities they serve. Police can do their jobs better when they have the trust and support of the community in which they work. Unfortunately, many communities view their police officers as the enemy. According to lawyer Sherrilyn Ifill of the NAACP, the relationship between police and youth in poor communities is especially bad. "By the time you are 17, you have been stopped and frisked a dozen times," she says. "That does not make that 17-year-old want to become a police officer." She thinks relationships between police and citizens can be improved by more firmly embedding police within the culture of the communities they serve. "The challenge is to transform the idea of policing in communities among young people into something they see as honorable," she says. "They have to see [police as] people at local events, as the person who lives across the street, not someone who comes in and knows nothing about my community."[58]

When police officers build stronger relationships with communities, they find it is easier to do their job, and the community becomes more supportive of the department. For example, Detroit police chief James Craig believes that his efforts to build good relationships have helped defuse extremely tense situations. Members of his community know they can trust Craig to tell the truth, whether it is good or bad. This relationship was tested after a sixteen-year-old boy was shot and killed by one of Craig's fellow officers when the boy pointed a gun at police. A video of the incident that circulated in the media did not tell the full story of what happened, so Craig personally talked to the boy's mother to explain the situation. "Looking back, I think part of the reason why there was no outcry or outbreak is going back to this circle of trust that was established," Craig says. "They knew the police chief was going to tell the truth."[59]

Reforms Have Led to Fewer Killings by Police

Research shows that when police departments train officers to reduce their use of force, the officers kill fewer people. Policies that require officers to comprehensively report on an incident or to exhaust other tactics have been proved to reduce police killings. Reforms like these should be implemented nationwide to reduce the number of people killed by police.

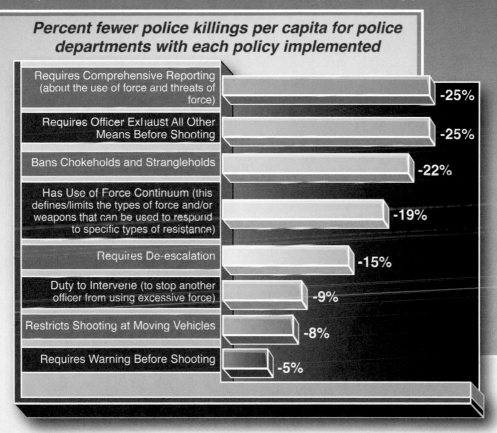

Percent fewer police killings per capita for police departments with each policy implemented

Policy	Percent
Requires Comprehensive Reporting (about the use of force and threats of force)	-25%
Requires Officer Exhaust All Other Means Before Shooting	-25%
Bans Chokeholds and Strangleholds	-22%
Has Use of Force Continuum (this defines/limits the types of force and/or weapons that can be used to respond to specific types of resistance)	-19%
Requires De-escalation	-15%
Duty to Intervene (to stop another officer from using excessive force)	-9%
Restricts Shooting at Moving Vehicles	-8%
Requires Warning Before Shooting	-5%

Source: Campaign Zero, "Police Use of Force Policy Analysis," September 20, 2016. http://useofforceproject.org.

Lessen the Focus on Force

In addition to building better relationships, police departments should de-emphasize training techniques that encourage police officers to use force. Many officers are too quick to use force, and research shows this is mainly due to the guidelines and training they receive. Seth Stoughton is a law professor and a former police officer. He says that training indoctrinates police officers to think their lives are in danger every time they go to work. "They learn that every encounter, every individual is a potential threat," he says. "They always have to be on their guard because, as cops often say, 'complacency kills.'" Stoughton reports that officers are not just told these things; such messages are reinforced with powerful video. "They are shown painfully vivid, heart-wrenching dash-cam footage of officers being beaten, disarmed, or gunned down after a moment of inattention or hesitation."[60] According to Stoughton, such training instills in officers a deep defensiveness and an instinct to use force, lest hesitation cost them their lives. As a result, officers become trained to shoot before a threat becomes fully realized, even though it might not be necessary to do so.

> "Policies and training on use of force should authorize only the minimal amount of force necessary to protect citizen and officer safety."[61]
>
> —Ferguson Commission, a group tasked with investigating the social and economic conditions impeding equality and safety in Ferguson, Missouri

This is why new methods of training are needed, such as the one described by the Ferguson Commission in its 2015 report. The commission was created to investigate the social and economic conditions impeding equality and safety in Ferguson, Missouri. Arguing that excessive use of force is both a constitutional and human rights violation, the commission advises a de-escalation of force wherever possible: "Policies and training on use of force should authorize only the minimal amount of force necessary to protect citizen and officer safety."[61]

More Accountability Is Needed

Finally, the US police system should be reformed to feature more accountability. When police officers do abuse their power, they are rarely convicted of a crime. In fact, it is rare for a police officer to even be indicted for breaking the law. This needs to change.

Consider that it is extremely rare for authorities to ever determine that a police officer is at fault for a shooting, even when there is clear evidence. This is the finding of research by Philip Matthew Stinson Sr., a criminal justice professor at Bowling Green State University. Stinson tracks police shootings and says that while it is relatively common for police to shoot civilians, very few are ever held accountable. "Millions of people have seen the video from North Charleston, [South Carolina]. Walter Scott was running away from police Officer Michael Slager when the officer shot him in the back, killing him instantly," says Stinson. "Yet after watching the video many times, a jury was unable to reach a verdict in the officer's recent murder trial. This is a story that has become all too familiar."[62] Stinson estimates that on-duty police officers kill approximately one thousand people a year; however, only seventy-eight officers have been charged with manslaughter or murder since 2005. Twenty-six were convicted of manslaughter or a lesser offense, and just one officer was convicted of murder. As his analysis reveals, police officers are rarely held accountable for killing civilians.

Community members are not happy with this lack of accountability or the many other problems with the police system. The United States needs to respond to this concern by making substantial reforms of its police departments.

Policing Reforms Are Not Needed

"Our system of local policing works well for the overwhelming majority of people, and we certainly do not need . . . to change it."

Dan Calabrese, "Obama: Hey, It's Time for 'Police Reform,'" *Canada Free Press*, July 11, 2016. www.canadafreepress.com.

Consider these questions as you read:

1. Do you think federalizing the police would increase or decrease officers' abuse of power?
2. How might you respond to arguments that suggest police and community members will always have an adversarial relationship?
3. Do you think the police system should be reformed? If so, which reforms would you recommend? If not, why not?

Editor's note: The discussion that follows presents common arguments made in support of this perspective, reinforced by facts, quotes, and examples taken from various sources.

Criticizing the police is common in the United States, and many argue that the system is broken and needs substantial reform. In reality, however, most of America's police officers do not deserve this censure. Former FBI director James B. Comey is one of many people who realize that although problems exist, the majority of officers work hard and do their jobs well. "Police officers are overwhelmingly good people . . . who took exhausting, dangerous jobs because they want to help people," said Comey in a 2016 speech. "They chose lives of service over self, lives of moral content, because that's who they are. They want to stop bad guys from occupying neighborhoods; they want to help old people off the floor and back into bed; they want to keep a young girl from a life on the street."[63] As Comey's words illustrate, most critiques of US police departments are unfounded. The police are doing a good job, and the system does not need to be reformed.

The Police Should Not Be Federally Controlled

Some propose federalizing the police, or bringing all police departments under federal control. This potential reform is not only unnecessary but could actually harm American citizens as well. Although some people claim that federal control will increase efficiency and accountability, the opposite is true. Clustering police departments under just one agency may actually promote corruption and groupthink, which is when a lack of diverse ideas leads people to automatically agree with each other, usually to poor result. Unifying control of police might also cause departments to be unduly influenced by one powerful individual or group. "These police agencies aren't very good at policing themselves. But at least there's the possibility that other police agencies might investigate them more thoroughly," notes Glenn Harlan Reynolds, a University of Tennessee law professor. "But unify all these police agencies under one umbrella and they'll do what guilty bureaucrats tend to do—hide the evidence, then investigate themselves and proclaim themselves blameless."[64]

"Unify all these police agencies under one umbrella and they'll do what guilty bureaucrats tend to do—hide the evidence, then investigate themselves and proclaim themselves blameless."[64]

—Glenn Harlan Reynolds, a University of Tennessee law professor

If the police are federalized, it will likely become an agency that does the work of the federal government rather than one that looks after the needs of people in communities. This is a concern of the John Birch Society, an organization that works to safeguard the US Constitution. "Police dependent upon the federal government have much less accountability to the local communities they serve," the society explains. "Allegiances become blurred and police serve the needs of the federal government instead of the areas they work."[65] Critics also worry that a federal police agency could be used to take away the civil liberties of US citizens. This has happened in other countries under totalitarian governments, such as Nazi Germany and Soviet Russia. As Jim Fitzgerald, the national field director for the John Birch Society, warns, "Have we so soon forgotten the Gestapo or the KGB, both national police agencies, that terrorized the citizens of Germany and Russia and led to the imprisonment and deaths of tens [of] thousands of innocent men and women?"[66] America's police have been put under local control specifically to prevent this type of abuse.

Community Policing

Some insist that police officers need to spend more time out in the communities they serve, getting to know the people who live there and building strong relationships with them. They maintain that this so-called community policing will improve police work overall. However, a big problem with the idea of community policing is that police officers and civilians will never have an equal relationship. Moreover, they will never have a relationship that does not include conflict. Thus, with or without community policing, there is likely to be conflict between police and community members.

Eugene O'Donnell, a former prosecutor and police officer, is one of many who argue that advocates of community policing are misguided in their belief that police officers can eliminate problems simply by building strong relationships with communities. In reality, he says, this type of thinking "blunts the adversarial nature of the police job" and erroneously suggests that people can have a conflict-free relationship with the police. However, if that were true, there would be no need for police at all. In such a world, everyone would obey the law. Since that is unlikely to happen, the nature of the role of police requires them to not be on equal footing with civilians. Consider a police officer who pulls a driver over and asks for his or her license. "Police are not equal with people in that situation," O'Donnell points out, "and you're not free to leave."[67]

The story of twenty-five-year-old Freddie Gray, who was arrested by Baltimore police officers and later died as a result of injuries sustained in their custody, illustrates why the relationship between an officer and a community member is insignificant when it comes to preventing

Reform Demands Conflict with High Level of Public Confidence in Police

Demands for widespread reforms in policing risk doing more harm than good, especially when polls show that public respect for police is at its highest level in years. According to a 2016 Gallup poll, three of four Americans say they have a great deal of respect for their local police. Even among nonwhites, respect for police has increased.

Americans' Respect for Police in Their Areas, 1965–2016

How much respect do you have for the police in your area—a great deal, some, or hardly any?

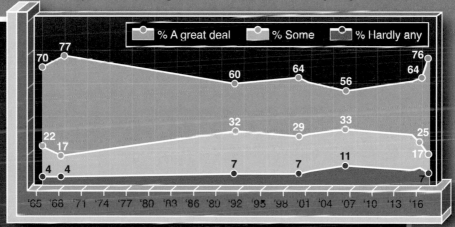

Americans' Respect for Police in Their Areas, by Race, 2010–2016

How much respect do you have for police in your area—a great deal, some, or hardly any?

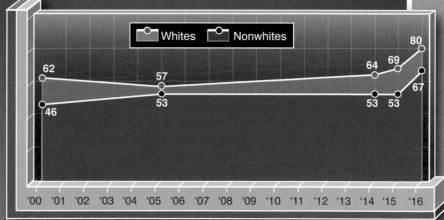

Source: Justin McCarthy, "Americans' Respect for Police Surges," Gallup, October 24, 2016. www.gallup.com.

conflict. Gray supposedly had a good relationship with one of the officers who arrested him, but this relationship between Gray and the police did not prevent him from being mistreated. "In the first trial related to Freddie Gray's death, Officer William Porter [one of the officers involved in the incident] testified that he knew Gray well and that they enjoyed 'a mutual respect,'" writes David A. Graham, who covered the topic for the *Atlantic*. "That didn't prevent Gray's death."[68]

> "As long as police know their badges empower them to operate with near-impunity, we don't need more encounters with them; we need fewer."[69]
>
> —Terrell Jermaine Starr, a journalist based in New York City

Another problem with community policing is that because officers are encouraged to spend more time interacting with community members, they actually have a higher chance of getting into a conflict with them. Terrell Jermaine Starr, a journalist based in New York City, notes, "In communities like mine, the predominately black Bedford-Stuyvesant neighborhood of Brooklyn, putting more officers on patrol doesn't lessen the chance of police brutality—it worsens it. As long as police know their badges empower them to operate with near-impunity, we don't need more encounters with them; we need fewer."[69]

Broken-Windows Policing

Another reform that has been suggested by critics is to eliminate a policing style known as broken-windows policing. It is based on the idea that when police prevent minor crimes in a neighborhood, they will also end up preventing major crimes. The name stems from the idea that when a building window is broken and nobody fixes it, it sends the message that nobody cares; this negligence actually encourages more people to break more windows. In the same way, it is argued that if police do not make a serious effort to prevent even minor offenses, then community members will get the message that nobody cares and will start engaging in more serious offenses.

Critics dislike broken-windows policing because they believe it leads to overpolicing in minority communities. However, there is evidence that broken-windows policing is actually extremely effective; eliminating this strategy would likely lead to more crime. Departments that use this strategy frequently report that it significantly reduces crime. For example, Louis Anemone, the former chief of the New York Police Department, offers an example of how investigating a smaller crime led to the discovery of a larger one. "I remember an occasion, when I was a lieutenant policing the relatively crime free Upper East Side at 4 a.m., when I heard a loud radio playing on a side street off Second Avenue," he says. "I knew the community complained about noise and noisy parties incessantly. I decided to investigate and not to drive on by. By stopping, questioning and frisking the youth with the radio I found out that he and three other youths had invaded a home and raped a young mother of two. I arrested all three youths."[70]

Across the United States, hundreds of police officers like Anemone are doing a good job, and their stories prove that calls for change are unfounded. The US police system does not need to be reformed.

Source Notes

Overview: The Power of the Police

1. President's Task Force on 21st Century Policing, *Final Report of the President's Task Force on 21st Century Policing*, Community Oriented Policing Services, May 2015. https://cops.usdoj.gov.
2. Barack Obama, "Statement by the President," White House, December 20, 2014. https://obamawhitehouse.archives.gov.
3. Quoted in Martin Kaste, "For Police, a Debate over Force, Cop Culture, and Confrontation," NPR, September 15, 2014. www.npr.org.
4. Philip Matthew Stinson, "Cops Shoot and Kill Someone About 1,000 Times a Year. Few Are Prosecuted. What Can Be Done?," *Los Angeles Times*, December 15, 2016. www.latimes.com.
5. Sanjay Sanghoee, "Why We Should Respect Law Enforcement," *Huffington Post*, December 22, 2014. http://www.huffingtonpost.com.
6. American Civil Liberties Union, "Police Excessive Force." www.aclu.org.
7. Eliott C. McLaughlin, "We're Not Seeing More Police Shootings, Just More News Coverage," CNN, April 21, 2015. www.cnn.com.
8. Quoted in Michael S. Schmidt, "F.B.I. Director Speaks Out on Race and Police Bias," *New York Times*, February 12, 2015. www.nytimes.com.

Chapter One: Do US Police Abuse Their Power?

9. Rosa Brooks, "America's Police Problem Isn't Just About Police," *Foreign Policy*, January 5, 2016. http://foreignpolicy.com.
10. Radley Balko, "Why We Need to Stop Exaggerating the Threat to Cops," *Huffington Post*, April 9, 2014. www.huffingtonpost.com.
11. American Civil Liberties Union, "Police Corruption." www.aclu.org.
12. Emily Ekins, "Policing in America: Understanding Public Attitudes Toward the Police. Results from a National Survey," Cato Institute, December 7, 2016. https://object.cato.org.
13. Philip Matthew Stinson Sr. et al., "Police Integrity Lost: A Study of Law Enforcement Officers Arrested," US Department of Justice, April 2016. www.ncjrs.gov.
14. Quoted in Daniel Bergner, "Is Stop-and-Frisk Worth It?," *Atlantic*, April 2014. www.theatlantic.com.
15. Campaign Zero, "The Problem." www.joincampaignzero.org.
16. Quoted in Steve Wyche, "Colin Kaepernick Explains Why He Sat During National Anthem," NFL, August 27, 2016. www.nfl.com.
17. Chris Amos, "An Open Letter to Colin Kaepernick," *New American*, October 24, 2016. www.thenewamerican.com.

18. Quoted in Garrett M. Graff, "Families Behind the Badge," *AARP: The Magazine*, December 2016. www.aarp.org.
19. Quoted in Graff, "Families Behind the Badge."
20. Quoted in D.K., "What the Cops Say," *Democracy in America* (blog), *Economist*, April 27, 2015. www.economist.com.
21. D.K., "What the Cops Say."
22. Quoted in D.K., "What the Cops Say."
23. Rudolph W. Giuliani, "Trump Is Right About 'Stop and Frisk,'" *Wall Street Journal*, September 27, 2016. www.wsj.com.
24. Sunil Dutta, "I'm a Cop. If You Don't Want to Get Hurt, Don't Challenge Me," *Washington Post*, August 19, 2014. www.washingtonpost.com.

Chapter Two: Are Police Biased Against Racial Minorities?

25. Jack Healy and Nikole Hannah-Jones, "Blue & Black," *New York Times Upfront*," September 19, 2016. http://upfront.scholastic.com.
26. Sharon Lafraniere and Andrew W. Lehren, "The Disproportionate Risks of Driving While Black," *New York Times*, October 24, 2015. www.nytimes.com.
27. Quoted in Alba Morales, "Why Are US Police Departments Still Race-Biased?," openDemocracy, March 16, 2015. www.opendemocracy.net.
28. American Civil Liberties Union, "Racial Profiling." www.aclu.org.
29. Bergner, "Is Stop-and-Frisk Worth It?"
30. Cornell William Brooks, Roslyn M. Brock, and Barbara Bolling-Williams, "Born Suspect: Stop-and-Frisk Abuses & the Continued Fight to End Racial Profiling in America," National Association for the Advancement of Colored People, September 2014. http://action.naacp.org.
31. Ronald Weitzer, "Diversity Among Police Officers Is Key, but It Won't Solve the Problems with Policing," *Guardian* (Manchester, UK), January 20, 2015. www.theguardian.com.
32. Quoted in Graff, "Families Behind the Badge."
33. Walter Williams, "Black Criminality Is the Problem, Not Racial Profiling," *Columbia Daily Tribune*, March 29, 2012. www.columbiatribune.com.
34. James B. Comey, "The True Heart of American Law Enforcement," Federal Bureau of Investigation, October 16, 2016. www.fbi.gov.
35. Quoted in Kim Christensen and Matt Hamilton, "California's Racial Profiling Law Is 'Terrible' Legislation, Police Officials Say," *Los Angeles Times*, October 4, 2015. www.latimes.com.
36. Alfred Blumstein, "In Assessing Police Racism, Note Racial Disparity in Criminal Activity," *New York Times*, November 25, 2014. www.nytimes.com.
37. Jamelle Bouie, "Black and Blue," *Slate*, October 13, 2014. www.slate.com.
38. Quoted in Bouie, "Black and Blue."

Chapter Three: Can Technology and Training Help Police Officers Do Their Jobs Better?

39. Quoted in Rory Carroll, "California Police Use of Body Cameras Cuts Violence and Complaints," *Guardian* (Manchester, UK), November 4, 2013. www.theguardian.com.

40. Matthew Segal, "If Cops Don't Turn on Their Body Cameras, Courts Should Instruct Juries to Think Twice About Their Testimony," *Speak Freely* (blog), American Civil Liberties Union, December 1, 2016. www.aclu.org.

41. Quoted in Martin Kaste, "New Orleans' Police Use of Body Cameras Brings Benefits and New Burdens," *All Tech Considered* (blog), NPR, March 3, 2017. www.npr.org.

42. Quoted in President's Task Force on 21st Century Policing, *Final Report of the President's Task Force on 21st Century Policing*.

43. Quoted in *Economist*, "Wanted: Cops with People Skills," April 25, 2015. www.economist.com.

44. Quoted in Cheryl Corley, "In 2016, Violence Pervaded Policing on Both Ends of the Gun," NPR, December 26, 2016. www.npr.org.

45. Seth Stoughton, "How Police Training Contributes to Avoidable Deaths," *Atlantic*, December 12, 2014. www.theatlantic.com.

46. Wesley G. Skogan, Maarten Van Craen, and Cari Hennessy, "Training Police for Procedural Justice," *Journal of Experimental Criminology*, SpringerLink, December 2014. https://link.springer.com.

47. Quoted in Jaeah Lee, "Why No One Really Knows a Better Way to Train Cops," *Mother Jones*, October 13, 2015. www.motherjones.com.

48. Robinson Meyer, "Body Cameras Are Betraying Their Promise," *Atlantic*, September 30, 2106. www.theatlantic.com.

49. Andy Campbell, "Police Body Cameras Aren't Helping You," *Huffington Post*, October 20, 2016. www.huffingtonpost.com.

50. Matthew Feeney, "Police Body Cameras," National Police Misconduct Reporting Project. www.policemisconduct.net.

51. Quoted in Peter Katel, "Police Tactics," *CQ Researcher*, December 12, 2014. http://library.cqpress.com.

52. Quoted in Philip Ewing, "DOD Defends Gear Transfers to Police," *Politico*, August 19, 2014. www.politico.com.

53. Quoted in Timothy Williams, "Some Officers Bristle at Recall of Military Equipment," *New York Times*, January 20, 2016. www.nytimes.com.

54. Josh Green, "Can We Train Police to Not Have 'Implicit' Racial Bias?," *San Francisco Chronicle*, October 11, 2016. www.sfchronicle.com.

55. Quoted in Joseph Erbentraut, "Police Department Bias Trainings Are More in Demand than Ever," *Huffington Post*, October 19, 2015. www.huffingtonpost.com.

Chapter Four: Should US Police Departments Be Reformed?

56. Brooks, "America's Police Problem Isn't Just About Police."
57. Daniel Lazare, "Why US Police Are Out of Control," ConsortiumNews .com, August 20, 2015. https://consortiumnews.com.
58. Quoted in President's Task Force on 21st Century Policing, *Final Report of the President's Task Force on 21st Century Policing.*
59. Quoted in Emell Derra Adolphus, "Detroit Police Chief James Craig Talks Crime, Corruption," *Black Life, Arts & Culture,* July 2015. www.blac detroit.com.
60. Stoughton, "How Police Training Contributes to Avoidable Deaths."
61. Ferguson Commission, *Forward Through Ferguson: A Path Toward Racial Equity,* October 14, 2015. http://3680or2khmk3bzkp33juiea1.wpengine .netdna-cdn.com.
62. Stinson, "Cops Shoot and Kill Someone About 1,000 Times a Year. Few Are Prosecuted. What Can Be Done?"
63. Comey, "The True Heart of American Law Enforcement."
64. Glenn Harlan Reynolds, "Reynolds: Want a Lawless Police Force? Federalize It," *USA Today,* May 3, 2015. www.usatoday.com.
65. John Birch Society, "Support Your Local Police & Keep Them Independent!" www.jbs.org.
66. Quoted in Alex Newman, "Obama Unveils Plan to Further Nationalize Local Police," *New American,* March 6, 2015. www.thenewamerican.com.
67. Quoted in Robert Siegel, "Community Policing Doesn't Sit Well with Everyone, Former Prosecutor Says," NPR, May 18, 2015. www.npr.org.
68. David A. Graham, "What Can the US Do to Improve Police Accountability?," *Atlantic,* March 8, 2016. www.theatlantic.com.
69. Terrell Jermaine Starr, "Community Policing Is Not the Solution to Police Brutality. It Makes It Worse," *Washington Post,* November 3, 2015. www .washingtonpost.com.
70. Louis Anemone, "Experience Shows That 'Broken Windows' Policing Works," *New York Times,* August 14, 2014. www.nytimes.com.

Police Powers Facts

Policing in the United States

- According to the National Law Enforcement Officers Memorial Fund, there are more than nine hundred thousand sworn law enforcement officers serving in the United States, about 12 percent of whom are women.
- The National Law Enforcement Officers Memorial Fund reports that in 2015 there were 51,548 assaults against law enforcement officers that resulted in 14,453 injuries.
- According to the most recent estimate by the Bureau of Justice Statistics, in 2013 there were more than twelve thousand local police departments operating in the United States.
- In a 2016 poll of almost eight thousand police officers, the Pew Research Center found that 58 percent said they often or nearly always feel proud of their work.

Use of Force and Abuse of Power

- A 2014 poll by the Roper Center for Public Opinion Research found that more than twice as many whites as African Americans said that they were very or somewhat confident that police are held accountable for their actions.
- In a 2016 survey of police officers, the Cato Institute found that 72 percent of police officers have never fired their weapon while on duty, except during required training.
- According to a 2015 report by the Bureau of Justice Statistics, between 2002 and 2011 almost 75 percent of people who said they had forceful contact with the police described the force as excessive.
- According to a report submitted to the US Department of Justice in 2016, between 2005 and 2011 police officers were arrested for crimes at a rate of less than one in every one thousand officers.

- According to a 2015 report by the Bureau of Justice Statistics, between 2002 and 2011 almost 44 million US residents ages sixteen and older had face-to-face contact with the police, and force was used or threatened on 715,500 of them.
- In a 2016 poll of almost eight thousand police officers by the Pew Research Center, 44 percent said that some people can be brought to reason only through physical force.

Racial Bias and Policing

- According to a 2014 report by the NAACP, only thirty US states have some type of law that addresses racial profiling.
- A 2016 study of racial differences in the use of police force, published by the National Bureau of Economic Research, found that African Americans and Hispanics are 50 percent more likely than whites to have an interaction with the police that involves the use of force.
- The US Department of Justice reports that in 2013 approximately 27 percent of local police officers were members of a racial or ethnic minority, compared to only 15 percent in 1987.
- According to the *Washington Post*, of the 987 fatal police shootings that occurred in 2015, African Americans made up 26 percent of the victims and whites made up 50 percent.
- According to an analysis of Gallup polling data from 2013, 2014, and 2015, 60 percent of whites rate the honesty of police officers highly, but only 28 percent of African Americans do.

Police Reforms

- A poll taken by the Cato Institute and YouGov in 2016 found that 89 percent of those polled support the use of body cameras, and 68 percent believe police need additional training to properly deal with confrontations.
- The US Department of Justice reports that in 2013 approximately seven of ten local police departments had a mission statement that included the concept of community policing.

- A 2015 Gallup poll found that 23 percent of those surveyed said they would like to see a larger police presence in their local area; 9 percent said they would like to see a smaller presence; and 68 percent said they did not want a change.
- According to the US Department of Justice, in 2013 the majority of US police departments that serve ten thousand or more residents trained new recruits in community policing skills.

Related Organizations and Websites

American Civil Liberties Union
125 Broad St., 18th Floor
New York, NY 10004
website: www.aclu.org

The American Civil Liberties Union works to preserve individual rights and liberties in the United States. Its website contains a blog, news, and reports about police corruption, militarization, and use of excessive force.

Bureau of Justice Statistics
810 Seventh St. NW
Washington, DC 20531
website: www.bjs.gov

The Bureau of Justice Statistics is a part of the US Department of Justice. Its job is to collect, analyze, and disseminate information about crime in the United States. The bureau's website contains numerous reports about crime in the United States.

Campaign Zero
www.joincampaignzero.org/#vision

Campaign Zero believes that the police should never be responsible for the death of US citizens. Its website has reports and policy statements about police training, demilitarization, the broken-windows theory of policing, and other topics.

Cato Institute

1000 Massachusetts Ave. NW
Washington, DC 20001-5403
website: www.cato.org

The Cato Institute is a public policy research organization dedicated to preserving individual liberty. Its website has articles and policy papers about various police reforms, including the use of body cameras.

National Association of Police Organizations

317 S. Patrick St.
Alexandria, VA 22314
website: www.napo.org

The National Association of Police Organizations is a coalition of police unions and associations in the United States. It works to advance the interests of the country's law enforcement officers. Its website contains news and information about police-related topics.

National Institute of Justice

810 Seventh St. NW
Washington, DC 20531
website: www.nij.gov

The National Institute of Justice is an agency of the US Department of Justice. It works to research and evaluate issues related to justice in the United States, in order to reduce crime and advance justice. Its website contains statistics and reports about policing and crime in the United States.

National Sheriffs' Association

1450 Duke St.
Alexandria, VA 22314
website: www.sheriffs.org

The National Sheriffs' Association works to help sheriffs, police officers, and others in the criminal justice field to perform their jobs in the best way possible. Its website contains a blog, news releases, and a library of publications related to law enforcement in the United States.

#ThisStopsToday

website: www.thisstopstoday.org

#ThisStopsToday is a collaboration of different groups who believe that police abuse of power in the United States is a problem that needs to be addressed. It is opposed to the broken-windows strategy of policing. Its website contains information about cases of police misbehavior in the United States.

For Further Research

Books

Stephen Egharevba, *Police Brutality, Racial Profiling, and Discrimination in the Criminal Justice System*. Hershey, PA: IGI Global, 2017.

Ana Muñiz, *Police, Power, and the Production of Racial Boundaries*. New Brunswick, NJ: Rutgers University Press, 2015.

Jeff Pegues, *Black and Blue: Inside the Divide Between the Police and Black America*. Amherst, NY: Prometheus, 2017.

John W. Whitehead, *A Government of Wolves: The Emerging American Police State*. New York: SelectBooks, 2013.

Naomi Zack, *White Privilege and Black Rights: The Injustice of U.S. Police Racial Profiling and Homicide*. Lanham, MD: Rowman & Littlefield, 2015.

Internet Sources

Radley Balko, "Why We Need to Stop Exaggerating the Threat to Cops," *Huffington Post*, April 9, 2014. www.huffingtonpost.com/2013/04/09/police-shootings_n_3038938.html.

Daniel Bergner, "Is Stop-and-Frisk Worth It?," *Atlantic*, April 2014. www.theatlantic.com/magazine/archive/2014/04/Is-Stop-And-Frisk-Worth-It/358644.

Rosa Brooks, "America's Police Problem Isn't Just About Police," *Foreign Policy*, January 5, 2016. http://foreignpolicy.com/2016/01/05/americas-police-problem-isnt-just-about-police-guns-violence.

Economist, "Wanted: Cops with People Skills," April 25, 2015. www.economist.com/news/united-states/21649507-when-law-enforcement-just-about-force-people-are-killed-wanted-cops-people-skills.

Emily Ekins, *Policing in America: Understanding Public Attitudes Toward the Police. Results from a National Survey*, Cato Institute, December 7, 2016. https://object.cato.org/sites/cato.org/files/pubs/pdf/policing-in-am erica-1-3-17.pdf.

David A. Graham, "What Can the U.S. Do to Improve Police Account-ability?," *Atlantic*, March 8, 2016. www.theatlantic.com/politics/archive /2016/03/police-accountability/472524.

Eliott C. McLaughlin, "We're Not Seeing More Police Shootings, Just More News Coverage," CNN, April 21, 2015. www.cnn.com/2015/04 /20/us/police-brutality-video-social-media-attitudes.

Michael Medved, "Slow Down, Police Are the Good Guys," column, *USA Today*, August 21, 2014. www.usatoday.com/story/opinion/2014 /08/21/police-militarization-ferguson-crime-violence-justice-bureau -column/14307505.

National Institute of Justice, "Police Integrity," June 27, 2016. www.nij .gov/topics/law-enforcement/legitimacy/Pages/integrity.aspx.

President's Task Force on 21st Century Policing, *Final Report of the Presi-dent's Task Force on 21st Century Policing*, Office of Community Oriented Policing Services, May 2015. https://cops.usdoj.gov/pdf/taskforce/task force_finalreport.pdf.

Seth Stoughton, "How Police Training Contributes to Avoidable Deaths," *Atlantic*, December 12, 2014. www.theatlantic.com/national /archive/2014/12/police-gun-shooting-training-ferguson/383681.

Index

About the Author

Andrea C. Nakaya, a native of New Zealand, holds a bachelor's degree in English and a master's degree in communications from San Diego State University. She has written and edited numerous books and articles on current issues. She currently lives in Encinitas, California, with her husband and their two children, Natalie and Shane.